What Became My Grieving Ceremony

What Became My Grieving Ceremony

Cara-Lyn Morgan

thistledown press

Thistledown Press Ltd.
410 2nd Avenue North
Saskatoon, Saskatchewan, S7K 2C3
www.thistledownpress.com

Library and Archives Canada Cataloguing in Publication

Morgan, Cara-Lyn, author
What became my grieving ceremony / Cara-Lyn Morgan.
Poems.
ISBN 978-1-927068-84-7 (pbk.)

I. Title.

PS8626.O7438W43 2014 C811'.6 C2014-900746-9

Cover and book design by Jackie Forrie
Printed and bound in Canada

Canada Council for the Arts
Conseil des Arts du Canada

Canadian Heritage
Patrimoine canadien

Thistledown Press gratefully acknowledges the financial assistance of the Canada Council for the Arts, the Saskatchewan Arts Board, and the Government of Canada through the Canada Book Fund for its publishing program.

For my family, the Morgans, the Monkmans,
the Brochus, the Kanes

I kept writing and rewriting, drawing and redrawing, and rethinking
and revising and reediting.
It became my grieving ceremony.

— Sherman Alexie, *The Absolutely True Diary of a*
Part-Time Indian

Contents

There Are As Many Words As There Are Blackberries

Ee-Matut

Bird of Paradise

Trinidad and Tobago

It rims the sky. The blue macaw, banana tree,
the stain of scarlet ibis, beak splayed open
to loosen a plum, pointed tongue. It perfumes
with cocoa, green coffee,
mahogany tree, plantain blossom, the metallic
blood of captured people.

A history built in the shuffle-clink
of chains on the ankles of men. Petals winging
in the dry season.

The leaves chewed
between the polished teeth
of missionaries, men who brought shoes and flu
and corsets to the people. Plucked
from the jungle, placed in a mason jar
where the sun illumined its yellow feathers,
its clipped, quiet stem.

(my grandfather's flower)

The Old Names

From Genesis to Revelations

The chair is too big, her feet spread out
from the fat cushion. She is like Alice, in a dress
that grows bigger and bigger around her. The house too
expands. The walls vine skyward, the curtains
spool upward in spirals of cotton. Inside her father's
house, everything dwarfs her.

Tonight she suspects her father
is listening. She voices
one demand. *Tell me the stories.*

She is the fine lines crowing
from the skin around his eyes, the fault
lines ridging his forehead, the puckered lines
along his top lip. The feathering
of skin at his collar, and every
frown line spells her name.

I need to know who I come from.

They have never before sat this way—angled
in plush chairs, a stand of books
piled casually between them. The past was high noon,
the span of polished table separating them, the Gary Cooper stare,
father and daughter waiting for the first obliterating draw.
Blood. Pleating of a defeated body. The agonized forward
crawling of time. Tonight they could look

at each other if they wanted. She watches
the airy skim of her socks above the carpet.
He watches the curl of steam from his lavender tea.
Tell, she says. He is an old man
now and the swelled droop

of skin beneath her eyes. The Indian
burn of fingernail marks across the tender map
of her inner arms. His name is scrabbled in the patchwork
of scars down her calves.

There are no stories, he insists. *I have nothing.*
He shows his palms, empty. To him, these stories
invite tenderness, and sadness—the thing
they already share. *There are no stories.* He chants this,

and she holds his hands
in hers, accidental, like strangers
who bump on the subway. Their palms have

never touched. The room shrinks
around her. The walls tip back from the floorboards,
the curtains suck back to the lung of the open window. Alice,
breaker of riddles. *There are.* She knows. *There are.*

Daughter

The wolverine cub, thick
hide, oiled hair and cuspate
claws, bites

and rips
without regard. Bleeds
moose, bounds
into this iced river to drink
and snarls
at her own reflection.

Tiger Lily

Saskatchewan

Against the dry prairie grass, a shock
of colour; blood
on the back of the white buffalo. A yearling's hide
dappled and downy, buckled
beneath the blades of the rolling combine, crushed
by the thick wheels of the Red River cart.

Petals cooked
into tea by medicine men to settle
wombs and quell dreams.

Plucked
from the fields outside
Qu'Apelle Indian School,
it shivered in its glass bottle
to the serial beat
of bedsprings
and strappings.

(my grandmother's flower)

Le Coeur de Laurél

For Grandma Kane

Use your latex finger to nudge the lungs
aside, expose the twist of arteries meshed
over gathered trachea, a picket fence
protecting the pull and release of the final breath.

Run the scalpel down the outer wall
of the coronary sulcas and slice free a heavy wedge
of birthday cake. Laurél's last white cake
showed 86 in chocolate frosting.

Sniff your incision. It should smell like a handful
of frozen dimes, the tops of hammers, a hint
of ocean salt. A wet, saline mist puffed up
from the dark coulee you've revealed.

Deep inside the vortex of the coronary sulcas is the dip
of the interarterial groove. Find it. Here, eleven
babies with goldfish mouths clung to heavy breasts.
Patrick, Thérèse, Gérard, Kathleen, Jacquéline, Paulette,
Shelley, Daniel, James, Francis, Joanne. Twined
around each other, crowding the cavity like puppies
in a laundry basket under the basement steps.

Cut, cut, cut. Feel the trachea through the sponge
of skin. Cut the custard edge of the pericardium.
The scalpel should glide to the place
where Father Ed died, autumn 1976. Just below
in the right auricular, pictures of Ed as a boy, not
yet a priest, one lazy pant leg rolled up on his shin.

Press. Breach the cutline between the right and left
ventricle, spread Laurél's heart wide, two halves
of a mango on the countertop. Locate the terminal sulcus
and stick your finger in. Refer to the Line of Union. Here, the day
Laurél married Protestant Irish-Métis
John William Kane.

She wore a handmade dress, he smoked
a hand-rolled Marlboro. Lower on this line, the day
their daughter Thérèse married a Caribbean boy. Humboldt
1970. She wore a sequined pantsuit.

In the terminal crest—two of her eleven, gone.
Shelley and then Patrick, snug in the fibers
of the musculi pectinati. One girl, one boy, woven
together like strong brake wires. Pluck
the chordae tendineae: Christmas 1933,
a new plough horse. Summer 1941, brother Armand off to war.
Summer 1947, became a wife. Autumn 1947, became a mother.

Pluck, pluck away. Fiddle strings, unchorded melody
of passing days. And the final cut.

Within the creases of the coronary sinus, thirty
fat and freckled grandchildren tumble around
one another, fluffed towels in the dryer. Peer in,
there, in the nook of the fossa ovalis, you will find
me, behind my sisters and beside two cousins, tight
together. A braid of still damp hair. Stick your thumb in
and touch me, gently.

My father, sucking bones

Sucking marrow from his chicken bones, spitting
the splinters on the rim of a white china plate, he cracks
the knuckles of his index fingers, first one
then the other, belches quietly into his fist, eyes closed on
another place   a different table   a two-room house
    its rusted roof

the palm in neighbour's yard, a splinter in the meat of his heel
from shimmying its ragged trunk. Leotha, his mother, digs
it out with her eyebrow tweezers, blows soft
on the wound, her ribs hidden in layers of mother-fat
church dress, apron. Roughs the sand from his skin
with her hand, cuffs hard his small ear, *settle*
boy, settle. Shows the sliver, shaming his tears
with the click of her tongue. Her children all left home

young, four girls, three boys, my father. Strayed
fast from Trinidad   to Harlem   Boston   Rosthern,
    Saskatchewan   abandoned

the taste of fried doubles   buljoul   dasheen
turmeric   green iguana   and how Leotha delighted
in shark-and-bake on Sundays. And she, poor
and afraid to fly, stayed in the red-roofed house, a whelp
of aging bones   a voice
on a long, long-distance line. My father

breaking a thigh bone in his teeth
rubs his tongue down the cracked leg bone
and licks it whistle-clean.

Nkochíspiten, Nizáminen

I touch, I taste

There is my grandfather, his hair pressed
flat by an ancient baseball cap, eyes
hidden beneath the dusted brim. There,
he speaks to himself, saying,
"*dishinikáshon* John Kane." His breath
whiskey.

There, beneath his railway clothes
on the brown surface of his skin,
the apparent Métis plains, unsettled rebellion,
his mother. There she is, hidden
beneath the vestment of an Irish name,

Mabel, there behind the Legion bar,
banging the stained wood with her withered fist.
"*Awéna kéya*?" Her voice a cold brook.

My grandfather, his glass
to his lips. *Who are you*, her question. "I am
no one." He says this so his children
may never be called Half-Breed,
Injun, Buffalo Jockey, Squaw. Coal-
cutter, yes. Leprechaun, Mick, but
never Tonto, never Nit.

And the ghost, her hand on his hand
on his glass, says, "*Nkochíspitan*,
nizáminen." And a secret is swallowed
for seventy years. Here

is my grandfather, his hand on my hand while we sit
on the sunporch. I am his tenth
granddaughter, there are twenty
others after me. Times like this I wish

I was still a child. I would
wrap myself around his knees.

There is a fog from our breath, and
in the cold he says, "*Dishiníkashon* John Kane."
He says, "*Nkochíspitan, nizáminen.*"
I never was nameless but now I am named

Monkman, the old name. His tongue calls
back the words
I may never understand. But there are no
questions this morning, for the secret
is his. I have secrets of my own.

Mother

The final months of Patrick's life
my mother tried to make me eat. Enticed
with plates of homemade pasta, green pesto,
whole wheat rolls yeasty and
warm in the centre,
peanut butter on salted crackers,
coconut curry, and once
a whole chocolate cheesecake
with raspberry drizzle.

I tried. A few bites
in and everything tasted
of cancer, round and sandy,
the rough insides
of tumours beneath
a fatty shell.

She told me
we have to eat
in times like these.

The last year of her marriage, my mother
did not eat. Once the house
was wilted
and quiet, after I'd started
throwing up
to keep from going to school
should I come home
to my father gone.

My grandmother said,
you have to eat in times like these.

Tumour

I'm the one to make Patrick's room quiet,
flick the dimmer switch and drape
a woman's slip over his bedside light.
I'm the one who slurps up his platelets,
who sucks up his skin cells one by one
by sweet succulent one, wiping the drippings
from his lipids off my chin. It's me who rides
the wave of marigold bile blooming across
the toilet seat and down the bathroom tiles.
I am the fist in Patrick's chest, timing the rhythm
of his toothsome, tender heart.

Halloween Night

A hearse in the drive. Witches press
their faces to its windows and wiggle
the door handles, seeking
a glimpse of the dead.

Inside the house, my uncle Patrick lies
like someone sleeping, not dead at all.
When they came to pull the last tube
from his wrist, I wanted to lick
where the needle was. My mother touched
his forehead, the hollows of his cheeks.
She still remembers

the sound of his rubber ball against their garage,
.22s smashing green glass bottles behind the barn, his
clothes torn from playing in the old switchyard, how he drove
their father's Beetle into the salt lake
to see if it would float. I remember
licking unbaked cheesecake
from his fingers as a kid, while he drank
Lamb's and seven, and how he taught me to braise
a brisket of freshly killed moose. Halloween night, and we

are the undead.
My cousin Samuel puts his hands on my cheeks and asks, why?
Why can't we go out trick or treating?
I push him too hard away and he cries,
his clown face muddied in tears
and I feel better for it.

I drink whiskey from a weighted glass, eat
candy while my middle-aged aunties smoke Patrick's
stash in the upstairs bathroom and weep fat, slow tears.

My grandmother wears her rosary
around her knuckles like a weapon
but does not pray, thumb pressing the Damascas
pebble against her first and second finger.

And Patrick sleeps in the crypt of the hearse,
which the neighbours realize is not a prop.
They bustle their devils and demons away, but
the older children still sneak up the driveway.

Though I am the one with your blood in my body

Fr. Ed Brochu

At Patrick's wake, the uncles spoke
of your funeral, of the autumn
drive through the prairie, and I
learned that Patrick's first name
was Edward, and that you both
were buried in fall.

There is a friar here who knew you, clasped
your hand, your broad shoulder, who remembers
your laughter, and the news of your passing. And though I
am the one with your blood in my body, here
is this man who shared morning coffee, split
a sandwich, heard your confession. He tells me

you had a stutter and that your funeral
was on my birthday. What I know
are from times my grandmother spoke
your name, storytelling, said, "Eddie."
Tapped your image with her fingernail, nodded
as if you still lived,

the boy she had cradled. In the pictures
your sisters are always touching you, until
youth stretched you, your big arms
wrapping your tallest sister tight,
tighter. In the pictures you are always
smiling. Perhaps because you were a priest with

the boyishness of a man whose heart
was never broken. If you'd lived

you would have baptized me, heard
my first confession. Given me my penance
and washed me in the blood
of Jesus. You would have sat
at Patrick's bedside, fed him
his last rites, the Sacrament
of the Sick. You are here tonight

with my uncles,
pressed around his coffin.

My father builds an iglu out back

The winter before he left, he built us
an iglu in the backyard. Careful
walls, solid yet slick. Leather mitts pawed

round prints on the walls as he carved
the snow from the banks with a wooden ruler.
Each brick building up snow

and sky. He doused the roof
with the green garden hose, misting ice
so the inside would be safe.

In the dim quiet
we pressed
our down ski-suits together, wound

tight our three pairs
of arms and pink elbows, giggled
in delicious silence.

Those icy walls. The metal smell
of sucked pennies. Our voices alight
in the sharp air. Fog of breath

caught in woolen scarves. Through
the narrow windows he cut us the view
of the swing set he'd built in the summer.

Across the lawn, if we'd been looking,
we'd have seen our mother inside
the house, warm and alone
behind the steamed-up kitchen window.

Descent: She

comes home, our mother. Aged thirty-
three. Three kids, three
jobs. Thirteen years of marriage, over.

Weary of living
this way. Low
income housing, mould

on the baseboards. Childhood
asthma times three. Husband
off with New Wife. No fresh

cold peaches, no thick bloody
steak. No man to grill it.
Just unwashed

laundry, unshovelled snow. Three
small mouths puckered down:
it's your fault. Her

fault. Her fault.
She knows, takes
control. Lets no

food through betrayed lips, no
sweet cream or hard
wheat rolls. She can't stand

what she's become.
Her curves give way
to pointed hips.

He has won. He has won. He has won.

Father

a slow-moving sea star, he crawls
without stirring the tidal pool, takes
time,
at times appears unmoving,
unmoved.

Beneath each horned ray, an army
of tubed feet, frantic.

Beside my bed, this picture and one of Jesus

Colours, sun-bleached. My father clinging to the front gate with easy fingers, tangling himself on the hot-iron lacing, a boy waiting for the postman or watching the approach of a skinny dog up the road. His boyish, wide-toothed smile for women and snap-shots. In the background, a half-dead palm and his brother, Dennis, back turned to the camera. The house where they both were born, the stucco wall they kicked a soccer ball against and, beyond sight, the shed where Maggie the goat was slaughtered. This is the start of all the stories I am not to tell. The place where our grandfather cooked iguana in the kitchen. Where Uncle George beheaded a long coral snake with a steel shovel while it sunned itself on the pathway. The rolling lumber of prairie trains was replaced by the yowl of mating frogs, the sucking sound of black lizards scaling the roughened walls. This photo, the wordless story that remains.

Long ago, the picture of Jesus was worn through by my own anxious thumbs.

The old names

Laurél Maríe Brochu
Mrs John Kane, Mother
Mérè, Mama, Grandma
Great-Grandma

Therésè Maríe Kane
Mrs. Dr. Earle Morgan
Terry Morgan, Mom
Therese Kerr, Grandmother
Terry Kerr

Kathleen Ann Kane
Mrs. Clayton Cameron, Mother
Kathy Dymond
Aunty Kathy

Paulette Marguerite Kane
Mrs. Carl Seitz, Mother
Grandmother
Aunty Polly

Jacquéline Yvéttè Kane
Mrs. Gerry Bomersine, Mother
Grandmother
Mrs. Dr. Peter Dessins
Aunty Jacqui

Joanne Mary Kane, Mother
Mrs. Joanne Schaffer
Jo Schaffer
Aunty Jo

Shelley Laurél Kane
Little Sister, aged ten
A photograph

Reading this list of names, I find myself

stricken
An infant lost in the wild prairie
thistles and thorny grass
bloodying my skin. Tonight
li noosim
the granddaughter, I want
to relearn my tongue

I speak their names
a stumble in this tongue
I know, the *môniyâw* tongue
the white man's tongue
that replaced their spirit names
with bible names, incorrectly
spelled. I ask them to return to me
in the smudge of sage
let me not be abandoned

Ni nókoms, long abandoned, all
but these dust-soft pages
these blurred photos
stern, heavy women
I want to hold their black braids
like an ox-tether, I want
to wrap their woolen
shawls across my shoulders

I call to my body the whorl
of their old fingerprints, that they may
enter me like thunder, *li toñeur*
that shakes the barns
and flickers the lights

In my most quiet calling
I speak their grandmother names
the left-behind names
the only names that remain

Sophia Bird, born 1792
Catherine, second wife
of Henry Hallet (first wife
unnamed, called "Indian"), Catherine
daughter of Maríe Pruden
Suzette, born 1815, Clementine
mother of Catherine, who married
a Scotsman, Margrette Monkman
born 1832, Nancy Bird, mother
of Charlotte, dateless
Caraline Coté, born 1847
Mary Inkster, born 1848
come awake

Come awake Mabel Monkman, born 1853
my mother's grandmother
Mabel Monkman with the white bone lighter
who clipped horse-shaped barrettes
in my mother's hair

remember to me the warm salt smell
of bannock in the outside oven
the smoke of walleye
on the river stones
enter me like the poplar
fluff that whitens the roadsides
and covers the grass

remember to me
my spirit name
let me not be forgotten

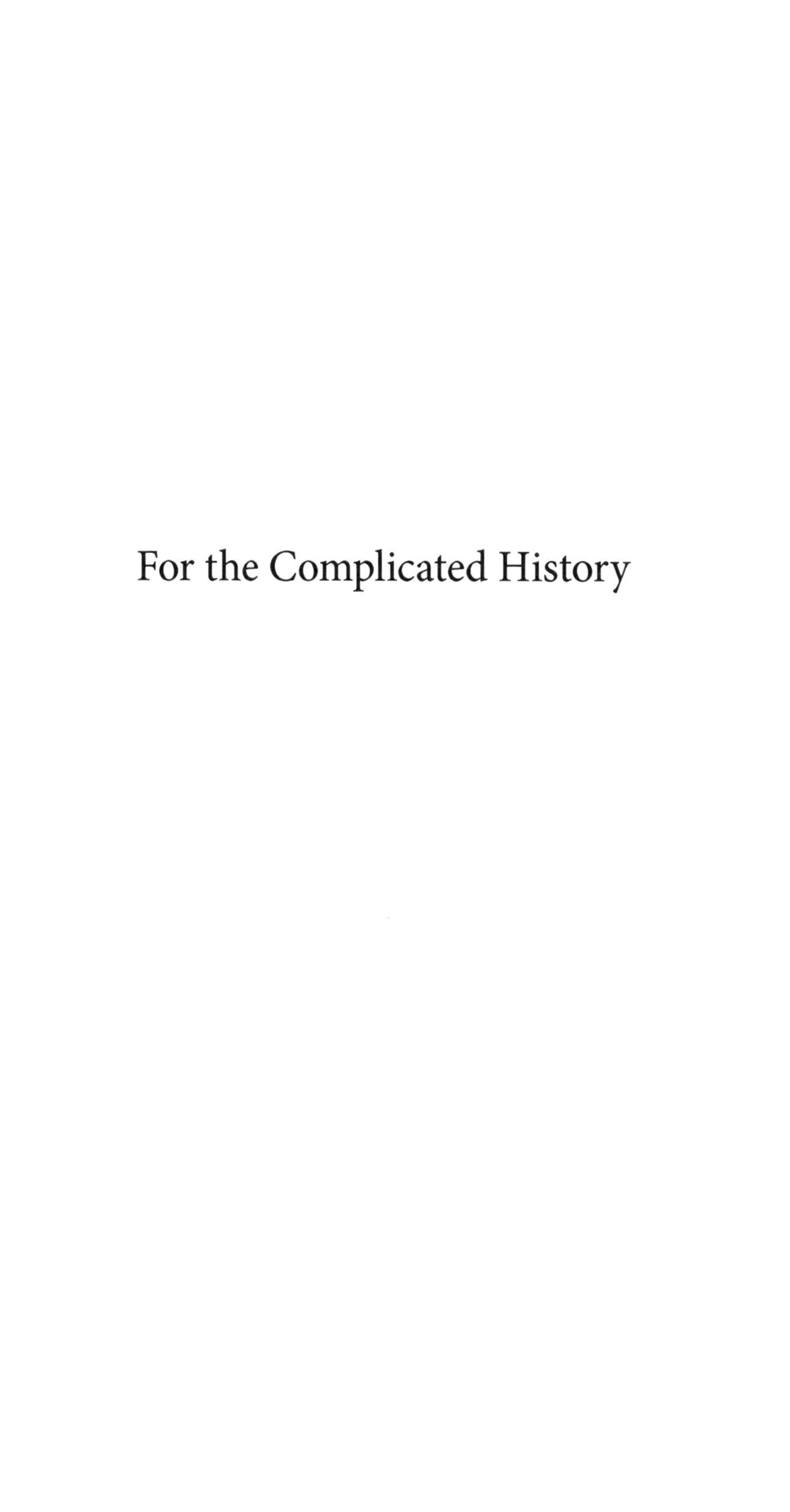

For the Complicated History

Speaking in a Voice Not My Own

for my father

How do I own   this history   cat o'nine whip   iron shackle
wooden ships stuffed with Africans   men aft   women in the bow
boys beneath the stairs   where the space is small   skin to skin   in
the dark   shamed   bought bought bought   to sit generations later in
diners where angry   white   faces   spit   only to be allowed.
How do I

own this history   that you   father
have thrust
upon me   to speak

of a terra cotta planter   smashed
on the garden stones   and

your mother   aiming   to hit
you   little barefoot boy   cleaning
shards from the garden path
so she   would not   cut   her feet.   How

do I   stand beneath
this history   Harriet Tubman   Markus Garvey   frigid blast
of firehose   bite   of police   dog through skirt and trouser   you ask
too much of me.   How do I stay

standing
drunk   at nineteen   still drunk
at twenty-one   bags packed
with your paintings   the Harlem Ballet
the Qunicy Jones   vinyl with   your name
on the sleeve   walking   away
walking   away walking   away from   your fathering
to keep my wrists   whole   you

telling
me   I had it
EASY

Telling me

tell

tell

tell

My Complement, My Enemy, My Oppressor, My Love

Kara Walker: silhouettes at the Whitney 2008

she cuts   black   cardboard sheet   boxcutter   black   paper scissored
from black hands   the vomiting man   crouches   shoeless
the cocked braids   of little girls   shoot like bullets from their black
heads   every   mouth   round and thick   each   tongue reaching
for tongue   a boy   chest stuck   out   a boat   slung from elastic
suspenders at his waist   as if a toy will bring him   from the
cotton fields   babies corded   still to their mothers   on the roadway
dangle

she cuts   the mothers   giving head   to the wigged massas   the
mothers taking it   in the ass   Uncle Tom   and   Little Eliza strutting
the yard   like black   hens   on skinny legs   another wall   clean
lined   silhouette   a woman floor   to ceiling arms   flung   skyward
wrists a fountain   above her braided head straight   razor delicate   in
slender fingers her bliss   and me   in   a room of projected lights
bits of blue and green and gold   on the white   white walls   my dark
shape   stiff   not cut-out thin dancing   black   against these scraps
another shadow riding   whitewashed walls

DIVER, 1962

In the library (thoughts of you) I flip
through a book on Jasper Johns,
wonder if I'll ever be good at anything
and whether you could love me.

Someone has dribbled coffee
on the pages of the book, stained
from the thumbs of other readers.
I learn a new word

encaustic, wonder
what you're doing now; sleeping,
reading, dressing for work,
thinking of the turpentine smell of my hair

wondering what I look like
beneath my paint-flung denim
and frayed t-shirt. Wishing me
beneath your duvet.

Someone has removed
DIVER, 1962 from page 95, left
only the detail, yet I am in love
with Jasper Johns and, maybe,

with you.
What would his walls of wax
feel like under
my fingernails?

How Do I Stand

a found poem

I.

To be sold
on board the Ship Adelaide on Tuesday
the Sixth of May Next: a choice cargo
of about 250   fine healthy NEGROES   just arrived.
          The utmost care
has already been taken, and shall be continued
          to keep them   free

from the danger
          of the SMALL-POX.

Wholesalers Austin, Laurens, & Appleby
S. Carolina, late 1700s.

II.

CAUTION!!! Coloured People
You are hereby respectfully cautioned
and advised   to avoid conversing
          with Police officers. For since

the recent order
of the Mayor
they are empowered to act
as KIDNAPPERS
And have been abducting,
   catching, and keeping
slaves.

Therefore if you value your liberty
Shun them.

Abolitionist Notice, Boston
April 24, 1851

III.

PUBLIC NOTICE!
committed
to the custody of the sheriff
as a runaway,
a Negro Man
who calls himself
Martin Barker.

about forty-three years of age
about five-feet-nine inches high
a scar over his right eye
and also one on his right leg, above his ankle

he states

that he once belonged
to Lewis Barker of Pope County

but now
he is free.

Advertisement, The Illinois Reporter
December 11, 1886

IV.

Ranaway
on the night of Monday
the eleventh July
    a negro man
    named TOM

about thirty years of age   five feet, six or seven
of dark colour;   heavy in the chest;

several of his jaw teeth   out
and upon his body   are several old marks
of the whip.
He took with him a quality of clothing.

A reward of $150   will be paid
for his apprehension.

Advertisement, The Virginia Gazette
July 12th, 1884

V.

The Origins of Urban Unrest
in Detroit were rooted in a multitude
of political, economic, and social factors
including
police abuse, lack of affordable housing,
urban renewal projects, economic inequality,
black militancy

Article, Michigan
1967

VI.

"Africville ain't no scar
a scar's somethin'that's healed
no
Africville ain't no scar
it's a sore. A sore
on the face of the city."

CBC Archives, Halifax
1967

VII.

Murder!

Eleanor Bumpas.

Murder! *Micheal Stewart.*

Tawana told the Truth.

Spike spoke.

Da Mayor cries out.

"you can't kill us

all."

Spike Lee's, *Do The Right Thing*
Summer 1989

Ack for me, chile, like yuh bin raise right

Leotha Morgan

Yuh puttin' on size granchile.
no man like a woman too big
to get tru de door,
no man like a woman big
as de house. Yuh gotta put down
de sweets
an take a walk.

I bin gone a long time
gone to see de good lord, an still, I got tings
to tell you, chile, before
I gone lay quiet tuh res'. If yuh
know to listen, yuh might
learn a ting or two.

Don' let yuh daughters be
tenderheaded.
Nobody like a tenderheaded chile
my gulls cry when I comb dey hair
whap! wih de brush,
dey be quiet.

Don' let yuh sons run de street.
Neighbours goin' tink you
dun raise dem wrong.
dey speak outta turn
use de cussin' word,
wine dey waist to dat soca
dat heeden brass
with dem local gulls in town.
Leh dem not forget, de lord
he punish wile boys.

Mah Milton bin gone
a long time, dis tru
he gone to see he Jesus
but I tell yuh dis:
yuh got to feed
de husband chile,
give him de curve belly

eh de man ha' de weight,

cook de pig feet long
to make dem tender,
soak de black-eye peas
in de kettle over night,
save de chicken bone
for stew. When dem babies
cryin for dey food
and yuh got nuttin
to gi' dem, remember dis,
inside de bones
is good marrow.
Cook dem long.

Don' wear dat hair nappy
wile, no matter
dat's de style. People
goin tink you don' kyar
how you lookin'. No
man like a woman
wit de kitchen curl,
no man like a woman
don' take kyar.

Chile, me gone a long time, dis tru
me gone to see Jesus
but my yellow grandchile gull
you still dere walkin' in dat cold
country. Yuh got to stan' up straight,
yuh got to go to church, find yuhself
a husban, a good man.
Don' talk so much.
Keep yuh eyes upward.

Yuh got to learn
to listen, chile. Ack for me
like yuh been raise right.

High Yellah

In the Big House, her daddy
was the Massa and she
wore the hand-me-down dresses
of the Massa's *other* daughters.

House nigger, never bred
for working fields, cotton
thorns, she was
the ornament of the
mansion.

Black hair tugged straight, powdered
skin fair and sunless. Hundreds
of years a mark
of the husband's
lust, she shamed
the white mistress.

Unkempt
bridge spanning a wide rushing creek. A bridge
that splinters in a palm.

Mule, bred
for a certain work, the work
of cotton sheets and
feather beds, sweat in droplets
on yellow skin. Worked
to exhaustion
and barren again and again.
No child ever hers.

She is still
the one with good hair
in the ghetto.

These Tears, They Do Not Fall

for June, who lets them

for the Cree wives of the Nor'west Company, rugged men
who bounced in their beds, brought pale-skinned
babies into wilderness homes, kneeled them
in makeshift Churches, then left. Returned
to the cities when winter was over, bellies
full once the buffalo returned.

For the Indian Schools' vacant
swings, the children beaten in the night,
their secret skin,
and the bibleless click of the lost languages.

For those light-skinned girls who learned
to pass, who cut their hair, corseted
breasts in whalebone, forgot
the smell of sweetgrass smoke, thick
pemmican on the tongue, and married well.

For the runaway slaves
inside pianos, pine coffins, feather mattresses,
the false bottoms of merchant wagons. The ones
who crowded the bottleneck
at Amherstburg, bleeding amid
the hunting hounds.

For those who sang
of the drinking gourd, limbs ice
in the bounding streams of Georgia, Mississippi,
who came to dry their feet in the soil of Ontario
and found Canada
a very cold place, indeed.

For the ones who worked the CPR
to own their land on the Bedford Basin,
and dared request the luxury
of running water, electric lights.

And so we drink down tears, river water
in cupped hands. Swallow them hard,
keep them like fireflies: if there is one
there are thousands.

These Times I Keep in Shoeboxes

For the cousins

Chewing honeycomb over the deep steel sink. Sun-warmed wax, thick
honey. *Cara, we're thieves.*

Moonstone beneath my sofa. Teenie said the universe wanted me to
find it, that I should keep it with me, always. The sound it makes with
my quarters banging against it.

Patsy, braiding feathers into my hair, tucking curls in plastic barrettes.
The clap of beads on the end of my braids. Her big-toothed smile
matches my father's as she combs through my tangles.

The wet-flannel smell of pee on sheets, and the promise not to tell
my mother. My mother, a whole summer later, unrolling the cot and
complaining that it always seemed to stink.

The boys, four-year-old twins, jumping naked in the upstairs bedroom,
bodies a blur from bed to ceiling, us girls in the doorway, peeking.

Patrick's van, us passing joints between long pulls of shiraz. Piled in,
riding the quiet, side door open to fireflies and cicadas. Someone lights
a big Cuban and we smoke.

The smell of skin, warm with sleep. Your hair tangled in my hair. Us,
cowered together in sleeping bags one dark morning, the sound of
coyotes in the barnyard.

The last day in October. Patrick's grave again, a year later. Michele
at my back, leaning forward, elbows hooked on my shoulders.

I didn't think I'd cry today.

No Long Time

Me and Patrick's ghost sit
here drinking Guinness and the sun freckles us.
On the balcony of that old apartment where
I don't live any more we are in the middle
of summer, a cloud
of marijuana smoke, his stash,
the best I've ever smoked, and the ghost
smells like the inside of his unwashed camper
a weekend after hunting mushrooms in the bush.

I tell him, Uncle
the family is asking
where you went those six years.

Uncle's ghost leans back, rests
his sandalled feet on the metal railing, *Girl,*
drink that beer it's getting warm.
I tell him they're guessing maybe
you went to jail. There's a smudge of dirt
on his forearm, and I wonder
about the smudge but forget to ask.

The ghost smokes his joint, slim and damp.
I tell him my theory: I think maybe
your heart got broken. He laughs
the way ghosts laugh. *Do you know*
hearts stay broken, even here? So it was

a woman, I venture and he shrugs.
Don't remember.
Did she die, I press him, and he laughs.
Death is funny, once you've done it.

And then my beer is finished,
the suns bellies the horizon. *Forget about it.*
Six years, he's saying, *is no long time. No*
long time,
the place I am now.

There Are As Many Words As There are Blackberries

This is the journey

The new fawn walks home. I stagger
through worry to gather the smallest
fragments of story. To hold them
as ash in my palms. Unwhole, fragile

a fragrant dusting of burnt sage
on my skin. This new knowing
that time runs out. That we are out of time.

Yet I do not know
how we will survive our loss of you.
Grandmother. You

the elk calf
nosing gently
in the shade
of poplars. Without you

the world will be less
playful. You
the wide prairie, the ripple
of wind in the long grass. Without
the frame of your bones
caging my hand, I may forget
to pray.

And what of these moments, these afternoons

drinking tea with Grandma Laurél

You pull out drawers of old photos, so old
they curl like petals in your palm. You are telling me stories.
Uncle Aìme and the eight-horse hitch. Father Ed's
church in Colonsay, the first gas-run tractor,
men building the barn, 1920.

In one, you bend forward, my infant mother gripping
your index fingers as she learns to walk. The baby's face
looking down at unsteady feet, concerned. Patrick, kneeling
in the doorway, smiling. Back when it was the four of you.
You were beautiful. You say, handing over a photo
of my great-grandfather and you on a railway platform,
These were some of my happiest times.

It wasn't the tears that I lacked

but the words. The words to name this mourning.
Should I speak for a family's grieving? I am as useless
as Eve in the garden, my fingertip on the curved forehead
of a calf. Warm brown head, fringe of curled lashes. Saying,
"You are a calf." The calf never answers
because I do not speak his language
and he cannot speak mine. Yet he feels the impress
of my finger on the strong bones of his skull.

He swings his head, turns on unsteady
legs, no more a calf
than a raven. No matter
that I have named him. So how
in my lost language, in my empty apartment,
in my brown skin, can I speak our sorrow? What
word in Michif captures the wail
at the hollow of my throat? How do I heal past
the rhythm of slave songs? The theft
of liberty, skin pulling off
the meat of the back. I will collapse
beneath the weight of namelessness. In writing
this, I am as useless
as Eve, fingering the caragana. Saying "Caragana"
as if saying it could make it grow.

Here on this old prairie,
I kick off my elk-skin shoes

I recall myself to these dry grasses. How
as a child I hated the prick of them
on my skin, and now I am a barefoot woman.
My mother is barefoot too. I know
without seeing, these bluffs are rich with owls, the ground
with bones and prairie-dogs nesting. Here, the valley
begins without warning. We tumble
into its sucking mouth.

My mother's hair
loses its curl on the prairie, falls flat
and long as in her youth, reaching
toward the grass. I feel the uncurling
of my own wild masses, my body
stretching in the seething wind.

Prayer to recover the lost names

for the grandmother ancestors, for Louise Bernice Halfe

let me call the sun *li salay*
and the earth *paskwâwaskî*

when it is snowing
let me say *mishpoun*

and when the rain mists the alder groves
let me remember *kimiwan*

let me call the rivers *li sipi*
and the mountains *waciya*

let the prairie be *le prairíe*
and the pond behind the barn

l'ci-luck with the brown ducks swimming
let the brown ducks be *sîsîpak*

let the black bird be *cahcahkayoos*
and the black bear be *moshkwa*

when he appears on the hillside
let the hillside be *ispatinâw*

remember to me jackfish
and coyote and elk and crow

l'brroshå
and *mîscacâkanis*

and *wâskîsô*
and *ohâsô*

when I am barefoot
on the springbrown grass

let the grasses be *kapaskwâk*
and when the sky descends

blue along the horizon
let the blue be

l'blô remember to me
brown and gold

and grassgreen
l'shakkwalâ

and *oshaw-sonias*
and *l'vârr*

remember to me *sîpîsis*, the cold stream
were the good crayfish hide, and to my lips

the old names
the *wakomâkanâk* names

ancestor names, Laura
and Mabel, Laurél. Nókoms

let me not be the lonely, bending
foxtail, wordless and wild

But I grow tired

of this coyote life, silent
and so lonesome. The lurking
in hunched shadows, stealing
into farmyards to rustle sleeping hens.

My throat has grown weary
of its constant senseless
baying at each moon.

My paws ache in
the cold alfalfa, seeking
out a ring of warmth.

To order

A steel guitar playing rhythm in the station. Iron
tracks woven into a sash. And Patrick, smoking
in the kitchen car, the thick-oil smell of breakfast with the 8 a.m.
joint. The tunneled rockies, blurred mountains
owned by the train alone. Patrick, nerves constant as the railway.

The order: One egg
soft-boiled. Brown toast. Coffee, black.   A chef
would offer rosemary butter, quail egg. Clotted cream
in the coffee, a dusting of cinnamon. Patrick, merely a man

on a train. A train on a track. A track through a mountain.
The steel guitar strummed in the station.

He brings the meal himself, just to say. When he sets
down the tray, his hand brushes the hand
of the man who, strangely, sets his paper aside. A shy
hello. Patrick, always with little to say, serves

the coffee in a thick white mug. The decanter
stainless steel. Soft-boiled egg, the top lopped
off. Triangled toast on a clean white plate.

Weeks later, in the mail, a note
on a thick white card.

> *Chef Kane,*
> *No one has ever gotten it right before.*
> *Cheers, Pierre Trudeau*

Patrick slips the note into the pocket of his suitcase
and there it stays.

Two men, one train. A track through the mountains.
Tin guitar strummed in the subway, the echo
of a man's hard sole, as I wait in the empty station.

Keeping you warm inside my skin

Thread of legs on laps, arms braided in arms. The sofa
stuffed with bodies, for we have never liked to be alone. The little ones
rest their heads on our chins, tap sand-roughed heels
against our knees. They smell of juice and salt, grass and fire.

These are the longest days of summer.

The wake. Patrick bound, tamed in suit and tie. We are a tangle
of linked arms. Our grandmother hands out scotch mints
from her purse as Cody falls, suddenly, off the edge of his pew.
A mash of laughter pressed back to our tear-wet mouths, as Patrick lies.

We have seen the coldest days of winter.

It's true we drink too much and are often cruel. Have known
one another's beds and basements, bathtubs
and bathing suits. Our first cigarettes flamed and extinguished
in the old playhouse as secrets, lilted and quickly stubbed.

Yours is the skin I remember always.

Leotha on finding a husband

Don fine yuhself some Baa-John man, some chupid
cunumunu gun cause yuh pain. Grandchile
yuh got tuh fine a good man, God-fearin'
a man who gon be useful in de house.

Yuh no wan a man yuh cyaa trus chile, a man
dat *movay lang*, de Lord dun like dat idle tock. Be sweet
and keep yuh hair comb. Pray. Stay away
from de *mah-ko* man always tryin
tuh bring de fete tuh he. Meet he in church, chile.
Dat wud please me.

Yuh outta time, ear dis. In time
de tot tots go flat and the bam bam take size. Yuh vex
tuh hear me tell yuh dis, me know. Cyara-Lin

yuh got tuh find yuself a husban. I gettin tru?
Hair me dis. Dun try me with dat *mamaguy.* All de gulls
dun married by dis age. Had babies. Make a life for deyselves.

Gull, yuh got to let yuh life
begin. Yuh know yuh wun
be yung always.

These things I know

On the prairie you can smell the rain coming
for hours before it falls. Sunlight
settles in barn rafters, catches
thick cobwebs, flies, and dust. The pull

of my mother's hands
in my hair, a deep comb parting
a path through my curls.

Sweetgrass smells like shortbread
before you burn it. Snow

on the steep hill, that outline
of night. And the stars:
stars in snow and stars in sky. The lonely,
animal call to the stars after a burial. That winter

hush. Dandelion cotton. The steam
off the calf as she exits
the cow. Her sharp hooves

cutting the cow's backside,
the farmer's chain round her new legs. Body
swung like a jump rope
between farmhands to make her breathe, and
the weary cow licking her clean.

For Avaya Maríe, *aen pchi baybee*

the little baby

These are the words I can give you: for uncle, say *onk*.
Say, *mon onk* Cole, *je'taime. Mon onk* Patrick, teach us
to temper the berries, to pull the heads from fresh crayfish.

For aunty, say *ma tawnt. Tawnt* Teenie.
Teenie, *ma tawnt, een estwer kitachimon*? Tell me a story.
Ask for the story, Avaya Maríe.

We are the women who know where you came from.

Your smile will come from Charla, your mother. This morning
she cradled you on her breasts, moved your hair with her breath.
For mother, say *Mawmaw*. Say, *ni mama*.

Faith you will get from your grandmother, Pauléttè, who
wanted to be a nun, but became a wife. This morning she cried
when she held you; tears portaged through your cotton sleeper.

For grandmother, say *nókom*.
Laurél, your mother's grandmother, had a narrow waist and
hair that curled at her shoulders. She parted it left while it was still
long. She is the woman who held all of our mothers. Each of us fit into
the nook of her elbow, toes kissed up against her mouth. This morning
she smelled the crook of your neck, clucked her tongue on her teeth.
That brightness is hers. Great-grandmother, say *arriérrè-grandmérè*.
Soon you will understand snowfall, and lover, and cousin and barnyard.

You will learn sadness and heartbreak, forgiveness and sweetness.
You will discover as many words as there are blackberries. But for this
morning say the newest one. Speak these words with your ancestor
tongue, the heavy tongue, the one that sits thick
near the back of your throat. Speak first with that learning tongue, and
you always will know.

This, this is the beginning.

How long your bones are, compared to mine

Femurs, long and slender as an octave. Climbing,
always climbing upward. You are a tree
that locates the space between ground
and sky. That broadens the space outward
with leaves and branches, shading
the grubs and beetles living
beneath you — moss and mushrooms
among knotted roots. I imagine this in you:
a slouching arbutus, awkward
in its treeness. Hunched, skin peeling
in the wind of a rocky beach. In a forest, you

would be lonesome. The quiet would darken
you, the sky make your blue eyes white.
Some days you are too beautiful
for this place. Most days
you are nothing but a man. Someone kind
who held an umbrella above me
in an insistent rain. Your fingerbones

long between the knuckles. When we stood,
palms praying, you curled your fingers
over mine. Swallowed
my hand in the flesh of your hand. This is the closest
we ever came to kissing.

Thumbs. How to encapsulate thumbs? Yours,
hard and ragged, nails chewed. A sliver of pink
blood where the skin was pulled
too far. Mine, neat
and ink-stained. Tips bruised. Beginning
with the hands, if we curled

back our skin, sinew and meat
stripped from white metacarpals, yours
would be the slenderest cage
for mine.

This buffalo sage I have burned

Singed wooden matches and heaped
ash. I have opened the door
to the fierce snow, burned
home the sad memories
of my grandmother, the voice
of my dead uncle. I have burned
the residue of my lovers
their imprint from my skin.

Any news of cancer once
and again, and again. Opened
the windows and released
words to the streaks of sunset. Burned

home the rasp of my mother,
weeping. The first Christmas
following a funeral. Burned
in the news of a birth, a wedding.
Called forward

the great women in my marrow, memory
of people settled in the seat of my ribs. Burned
for guidance, received silence. The linger
of smoke in a room.

Even in my *moniyâw* tongue
words are but glass petals. Nothing
more than the scatter
of roaches when I flick
the kitchen light on.

I am restless, it's true
and impatient. I am not humble. I wish
for you to care for me
like an infant, swaddle me.
I am not strong enough
to hold myself. I have burned
frosty time, burned my own bones
brittle.

Michif

This pursing of lips. Lonely love-making
of language. Rooted, certain Cree touching
a warm slick tongue to homesick, lonely French. The tapping
of a man's teeth on a woman's
teeth. His breath: "*Dimanche.*" Her mouth:
"*Jimawnsh.*" Their tongues
adorned with kisses. Her fingers to the snowfall,
"*Mishpoun.*" Saying, "*Kishinaw.*" It is cold. His
chapped lips across her softest skin.

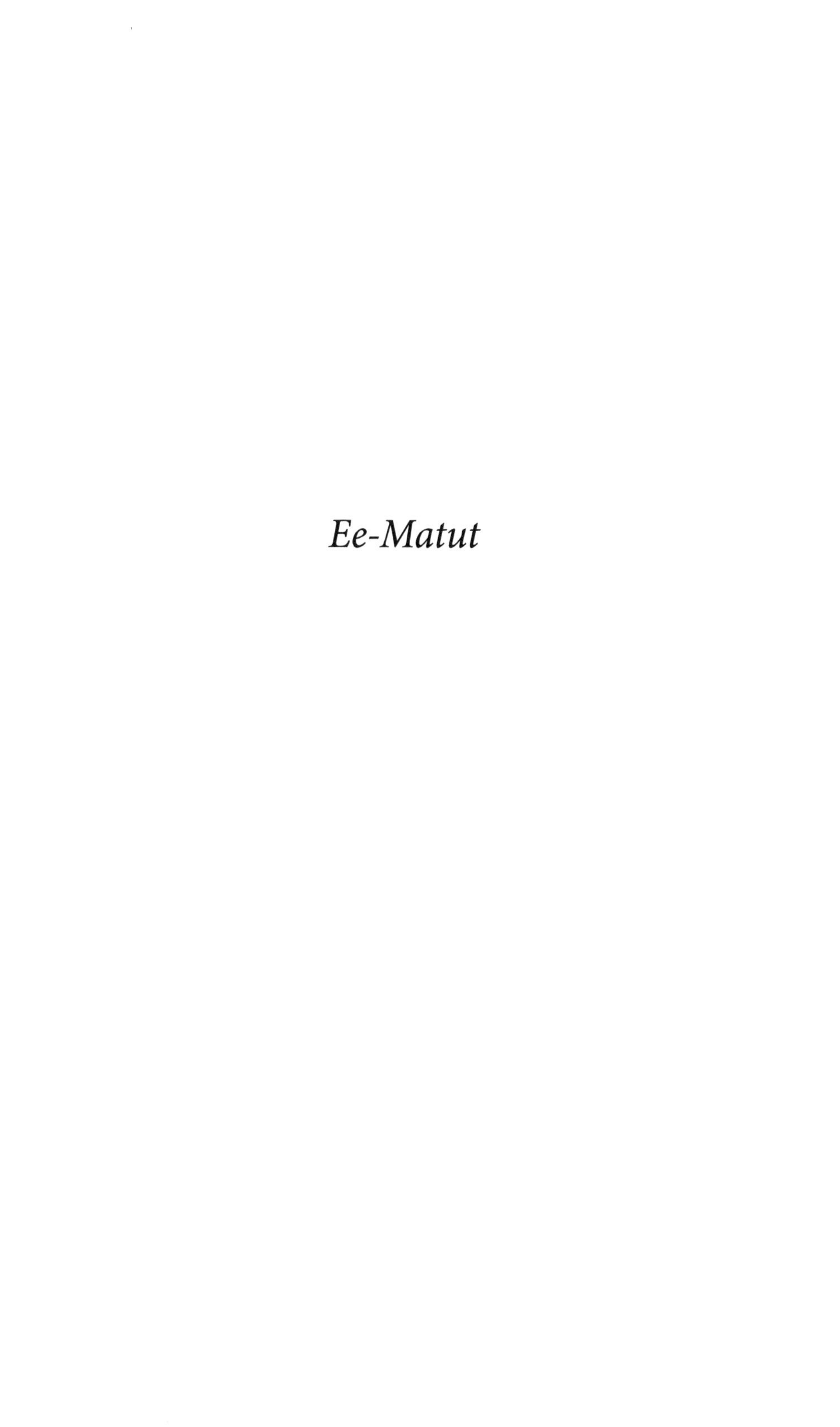

Ee-Matut

This evening in church, we keep our coats on

The snow on the skylight has darkened our faces and Mass is late due to weather. My mother, my grandparents, and the few others who have shouldered the snow are huddled together. There is no heat. I don't know this, but tonight will be our last service together.

I have seen the priest on the golf course. He favours a cigarette and a cold pint of Race Rocks. Tonight, he reads from the Book of Samuel:
I am living in a house of cedar.

Beside me, my Grandmother reads her missal. She turns the pages noisily, leans her purple goose-down sleeve across my arm and whispers, "What are you writing?" I show her my notebook: a sketch of the estuary scribbled sideways across the blue lines, stalks of wheat on Father's vestment. *Go, do all you have in mind, for the Lord is with you.*

She pretends not to smile, clucks her tongue. The room is thick with wood polish and smoke and peppermint. Father blesses us, *The peace of the Lord be with you*. He adds, "Today is the shortest day of the year. The first day of winter, the darkest day." I think of the snow pressing on the glass ceiling.

Draw the skylight tumbling in, showering the altar, the priest, the assembled, in a thunder of glass and snow and wood. The service ends, and my Grandmother takes my arm as we step into the street. It is a cautious walk, and I am her staff. We lean forward into the sharp, steep wind.

You took your own time

to die.   Your time,
no one else's. Just like you always did. Feral
as a dog-raised child, you refused the Catholic
confines of our family, came
and went when it pleased you. Always
so detached from the family, us kids
lining the chesterfield, watching the road for a billow of dust:

your camper, which sometimes crawled and bumped
up the drive, but mostly didn't bother
the farmyard with its dripping
oil nor you the card table
with the clink of your scotch.

There was a time I would not have missed you.
Would have counted your absence among
those of Great Aunties and Uncles whose dead old faces
I was forced to kiss at wakes. But you came home
in the end and wrecked it. My ease of losing you.

For two years we drank beer on the rusted balcony while I ignored
shrinking shoulders, the tripping
gait of your wooden clogs. Thieved comfort

from you in the kitchen, drinking Pernod
while you pulled the small black eggs
from shrimps with your radiation-trenched
thumbnail. We smoked joints
in the driveway, camper canopy open over the lawn.

Now I have begun to forget
your reddish hair swept left, the wilderness
of your clothes, there is a pulling
away. Shock of loss. Years have passed
yet Tuesday riding home on the bus, I

am weeping. The clatter
of traffic wet on my face
when I realize what I have forgotten:
my mourning of you.

They have seen these stories, they know

there are as many as hummingbirds, as streaks
of sunlight through the open window. In the evenings
I spy them: half-drunk
glasses of rum caught up. Our fathers
so slight
they appear to be just men falling asleep after dinner.

The stories spiral. How we became
lost, the daughters. Why we disappear like steam.

Maybe we were not loved enough
and they were not loved enough.

We do not sleep with their stories, forgotten
between these shores and the old ones, we daughters
cold and thin, in the prairie. Silent
as the hard-packed snow. Awake
in our husks of yellow skin.

You can never go home

I'm told that my granny's last breath came and went on the bend of
road in Trinidad where, forty years before, my grandfather's
bike tire hit a ridge that bucked him headfirst
into the pavement.

They are buried in the Adventist churchyard
and my youngest uncle brings them notes and flowers, trims
weeds from their headstones.

My father stood once in that graveyard, as a child
stands at the foot of his parents' bed, seeking
comfort from a rattling pipe, a whistling frog,
the chuckle of screech owls, whispered tales
of the *sucouyant* who sheds his skin,
then drinks the blood of the sleeping.

A child, waiting for someone to wake
and see him outlined in the doorway, nest
him deep in the covers.

They never woke. He stood
at the headstones.

Mother's Day

Today in Qu'appelle our spirits
return to the burial place of the ancestral bones
the place of our Grandmother's
ghost. A day for our mothers,

now motherless. No gift
to wrap, or card to sign. My mother
swallows her sadness, blows her nose
too loud. She will continue

to lay the table, rise the bread. We move
as a pack from brunch to gravesite
to evening meal. Hold hands
and sing before eating. Speak

to those gone before us, faces
to the graveyard lawn, the headstone. Daily
we wail our goodbye, our losses
animal at first, sputters of hard air,
then quiet as the passing time.

Today is your birthday, Uncle

My mother has baked
a pecan-rum cake. And we
are all drunk on whiskey.
Three days ago, she gave me
a red fleece blanket
for my birthday. I pushed it away
and ignored her tears. I am fat
with shame this first hoggish
year of living without you.

I worried through the toasts
that we might start singing. Ridiculous
in a cemetery, but then
so many things are.

The ground littered
with offerings, artificial flowers,
letters sealed
in faded envelopes, photos
curled and thick with dew. We

pour the last whiskey over
your headstone. I toe
the mud around your grave, as if
to nudge you.

Photo of Father Ed

Graduation, Seminary College

the day he ceased to be just Eddie. Cluster
of mischievous boys, grins wide and prideful, soon
to be the savers of prairie souls. Mothers
placed their faith in the palms of these young men, farmers
sweated out their secrets to them
through wooden screens. They are all gone

now and no one remembers
their names or knows
if their faith carried them through
to the next world.

There was a great party
the day they buried Father Ed, the friars
drunk on whiskey and pitchers of red wine. The priests
and family sang and wept and this became the grieving

ceremony, a wolf pack walk
from church to grave, the hush
of ending, amid the howl.

Family reunion, my grandmother

watches us with a tilted shyness,
sees a calf birthed in the barn,
a room full of babies. Spring
orchids up through hard winter soil.

Each of us she has held in the bend
of her elbow. There is no one here
whose tiny feet she has not kissed.

To each of us

she gives her fingers, the tender
petals of her thumbs. We gather these
in cedar baskets, float them down
the South Saskatchewan. They are
the infant Moses.

To her five sons, she gives
her rough hewn palms. The left
for cupping clean water. The right to cradle
blue dragonflies and ladyslippers.

At evening grace, we fold them together,
the left hand, the right hand. In summer,
make shovels to till the earth. At harvest
they are the cool husks sifting
inside the dark silo.

To her six daughters, she gives
her arms crossed on her chest. We sew
a great, strong sail, we move outward,
draw walleye to the boat's sides.
To her granddaughters, she gives
her dozen ribs. These we gather
like daffodils, weave their stems
through our heavy braids. They
are the trinity, the cleanest part.

To her husband she gives back the nest
of her womb, cradle for the eleven
who slid out like kittens, steaming
on white linen. To him

these are the cavities of the heart,
the story's end. Her fingers beneath
his chin the night she died. A shoeless
walk to the spirit place. Coming back
to the ones who've walked ahead.

We never sought to anchor you, Uncle

beneath pounds of sand. You ran
from home along a rocky roadside. Left
us waiting. Then

entered illness
and your tamed return. The soft
cotton washcloth
cooling your fevered face as you sat
at my table rolling joints
while I did your taxes, ten years
unpaid. A scatter of small twigs
and rocks from your sleeve on the tabletop.

You smelled of wet flannel, forest
fires and bush mushrooms. Hospital linens. The joints,
thin tubes lining the space between us like blinds hung
open across a darkened window. It was afternoon
and we had already drunk the merlot. Each swallow

the backdraft of time. The breath
between diagnosis and death. Each
moment between us a sea turtle nesting
pushing back cold sand with awkward feet.

And this, goodbye

I.

I know by our hug this morning,
this is the last I will see of you. Your life.

You are so small today
and so pale.

Your life ballooned in the middle
like the curve of a toddler's belly

then slendered out again
and you have gone quiet. The tumour

in your stomach feeds
on the nutrients from your food, and you

starve.
I sift through your photos,

picture after picture
gather names, places,

final stories, while your eyes
fade backward in time.

II.

This is all the time we get
from the woman who held us.

Because the first funeral is
the hardest and then they just run on.

The thing that amazes us
most is autumn. The cold

kettles in like a hawk,
unshy. Frost coats

the door handles. That miracle
of breath, in and out.

Blue crocus aflame
on a colourless stretch of snow.

Wake

Moss of frost on the half-open windows.
Mourners in a moist kitchen. The sting
of garlic, overlaid with rosemary, lilies. Men
in Sunday cologne. My mother
tugs autumn corn from rubbery husks.
How we speak

our farewell. Rosary bruising
my wrist. Tonight, the last of the merlot
coats our glasses, Kleenex is pulp
in our sleeves and pockets. The children
hang over the edge of the casket, *Her lipstick*
is too pink. They retreat to the basement
to play cards, watch tv. Up here
we are scraping food from plates into the trash.

Outside,
the flutter of new, heavy snow.

Mon onk, mon onk

my uncle, my uncle

Mon onk, tande pe'ootoyan?
The sky above St. Louis is starry and cold
and I wonder if I only imagine Heaven
because of my grief. From there, can you see *le cherañ*?
Are you arrested by beauty, even there?

Mon onk, een istwer kitaachimon?
I call up your voice, a sharp cool rumble
like handfuls of gravel in a ragged palm.
You told me once to learn the language
of our *nókoms*, our *moshoms*
so I could speak to the ancestors
and be heard. And now you
are one of them. *Mon onk*,

I think of you often
in the jazz club in Kelowna.
I was twenty and you
wore your navy sport coat.
You called Jesus through the music
and I was ashamed
in the room of quiet white people
                                        and envious.
Mon onk, in those last days
I wasn't there for you, was not
brave enough to touch *ta maen*. To sit
with you, sink my head
on your damp pillow. Answer
when you cried through the morphine
in our silent, sleepless house.

On your funeral day, I came
to the room
where you died, and began
ee-matut, to cry.

But the truth:
many nights I drank my grief quiet,
and asked God, often,
why he made
me suffer.

"Was call home"

The hundred-year-old woman leans back into
her wheelchair and locks bent fingers
across her chest. She has buried her eldest child.

"Firs' son," she tells me. "He jus' slip
away one night. Was speakin'
wit he bruddah and den jus' fell
tuh sleepin'." Her eyelids slip downward.
"Was call home," she says.

"Everyone love he so." Her words filter
through lost front teeth. "Muh lef muh tears
in Trin'dad, and now
is time to be wit' he and de family."

She and I know,
that is all. Loss,
a knowing
you have no choice
but to press forward
left foot before right. She tells me,

"Someday, you gonna be call
home too." Her crooked palm
tilts skyward, then she rests.

A hundred years.
The startled blooming
of the untrimmed poinsettia
that crowds the front gate in December.

The coming
of the rainy season
after the dry. The ibis cry.

Coyote

For Father Ed, St. Micheal's Retreat

How strange and yet unstrange that I should find
you here. That our paths have led
us to this place where you'd have been
most at home and I, among friars and poets,

am at home too. Maybe
it's that you were a coyote and I am a coyote.

After Patrick's funeral, I smelled him.
Caught his shadow.

Is it because today is solstice,
and we are orphans? Or simply
that the wall between spirit and living
is letting through the voices. I turn,
and hear you.

Let us remember the things we lost

when we were a wolf pack
baying at glass breaking in the garage from a stumble
across a field of leather shoes. That morning we woke
and were not lonesome, did not send out a silent greeting
to the air around us. Good morning to the dead.

Before the air was smudged
in sage, we did not mourn. Yet those we lost
knew loss too, fell to the kitchen tiles, fists
through cellar doors, death
swallowed with Bushmill's and ice.

There was a time before
the grass-covered graves
when the thing we had lost
was an eyeless doll we once held,
ugly, ragged, and worn.

For Patrick, years after

on moving from Vancouver Island

It's easy to leave, though everything about this island
reminds me of you; the filthy campers, braided smell
of pot and patchouli, twilight drums played
by men in the doorways of driftwood houses.
Today, I wonder
when did I recover? How did I learn

to leave you to the grandfathers, to Ed and Réné
and Aimé, to Armánd. Trust them to keep you
near us as they never could in life. Remind you
that we are the ones you walked forward without, watched
us as figures shrinking in a rearview, swallowed
by road dust. We stood at the gravel shoulder
and waved. Maybe we are most at home

being left by you. And maybe it is time now
to release you to the white buffalo and find
ourselves free. This is animal mourning, loss
suspended in the folds of our skin. Water
in a deerskin pouch. Now we must open

the windows and leave you. Release you to be
Coyote, Jack Pine. Barefoot
in an evening sky. Shadow
on a coulee wall.

Into this world

Lessons for my Godsons

Skim your hands
on dandelions, scatter
parasoled seeds. Spread

your toes in cold sand,
leave lakes on the beach. Palm
blue pocket stones, robin's eggs.

Chew the sweet roots of baby grass.
Lie on a hill, fingers
linked behind your skull,

let clouds shadow your face,
sleep. Wake to the sun
slipping

below the horizon,
as the secret dark
overcomes.

Only here can you begin
to see
the spirit horses.

Acknowledgments

I would like to thank the literary magazines and journals that continue to support and nurture poetry in this country, that champion writers amidst funding cuts and staffing issues and introduce new work to the literary landscape again and again. Some of the poems in this collection appeared in their earlier versions in *CV2, Grain Magazine, Prism International, The Antigonish Review, The Nashwa'ak Review, The Windsor Review, Other Voices,* and *Room Magazine.*

Gratitude and love to Teresa Taylor, Rhonda Batchelor, June Halliday, Katie Tanigawa, Laurie D Graham, and the wonderful John Barton. Your patience and support with the early versions of this manuscript encouraged me to keep pressing through. Especially John, who gave me new words and brought order to my poems. And to my editor, Michael Kenyon, who I believe is a coyote just like me.

To Tim Lilburn and Lorna Crozier, for teaching me how to stand beneath these stories.

To my family, those living and the dead, I hope I have honoured your voices.

And finally to Amelia, who loves so well.

Cara-Lyn Morgan was born in Regina, Saskatchewan and her family has been on the Canadian prairies for many generations. Her Métis mother is from Spiritwood, Saskatchewan, and her father came to Saskatchewan as a young immigrant from Trinidad. She is a working writer and painter and a graduate of the University of Victoria's Creative Writing program. Her work has appeared in a variety of national literary magazines. She lives in the Toronto, Ontario area.